student WORKBOOK

AS/A2 English Literature
Intertextuality & 'Connections'
Michael Fynes-Clinton

D1789240

Philip Allan Updates
Market Place, Deddington, Oxfordshire, OX15 0SE

Orders
Bookpoint Ltd, 130 Milton Park, Abingdon,
Oxfordshire, OX14 4SB

tel: 01235 827720, fax: 01235 400454

e-mail: uk.orders@bookpoint.co.uk

Lines are open 9.00 a.m.–5.00 p.m., Monday to
Saturday, with a 24-hour message answering service.
You can also order through the Philip Allan Updates
website: www.philipallan.co.uk

© Philip Allan Updates 2007

ISBN 978-1-84489-476-5

Printed in Spain

Philip Allan Updates' policy is to use papers that are
natural, renewable and recyclable products and made
from wood grown in sustainable forests. The logging and
manufacturing processes are expected to conform to
the environmental regulations of the country of origin.

P00906

Introduction

This workbook focuses on intertextuality — the way we can make connections between texts. The term has a particular critical meaning but in this workbook we are going to use it in its wider sense, meaning the way we read a group of texts rather than one text on its own. The workbook is relevant to all AS and A2 specifications.

The workbook is divided into several parts. The first is a long section, covering a range of different aspects of intertextuality, some of which are developed later. The rest of the workbook focuses on the role of intertextuality in the following sections:
- 'placing' a text
- developing an interpretation
- periods and themes
- genre
- grouping texts
- coursework
- preparing for examinations

You can use the workbook as a way of developing your confidence in linking texts during the AS course (although 'making connections' is not a specific requirement of the first year of A-level), or as a key part of your preparation for the demands of the A2 course. It is designed for you to use either on your own at home or with others in the classroom as a starting point for group discussion, presentations or research.

The A2 assessment grid ensures that all examination specifications require you to link, compare, contrast or connect texts. Specifically, you may be required to:
- make comparisons between substantial whole texts in order to understand and comment on what they have in common and on significant differences between them
- evaluate different viewpoints and interpretations
- synthesise knowledge and understanding of the styles, contexts and meanings of literary texts

This complex and demanding skill is assessed in a number of different ways depending upon the examination board. Here are some of the ways you could be asked to do this:
- through coursework choices, comparing texts through genre, period or style
- through questions that ask you to compare two prepared texts, related by time and period, or by theme or genre, or written by the same author
- through a comparison of a directed text and a free-choice text, with the addition of a range of wider reading, all related through period or genre
- through some form of pre-release material supported by your own wider reading, all related to a particular theme and ranging across literary and non-literary genres

All of these approaches focus on the context, genre and style of more than one text and, because they assess the whole range of Assessment Objectives, are generally (but not always) examined in the synoptic unit. They require you to demonstrate both breadth (range of knowledge) and depth (detailed knowledge and understanding).

The advantages of growing more confident in the way you respond to links and connections are:
- You will train yourself to avoid making generalisations that are vague and based on little specific knowledge.
- Since comparisons require careful focus on detail, you will develop the depth of your understanding of the way literature works.
- Since comparisons also require you to range more widely over several texts, you will broaden your knowledge and understanding.
- If you are required to respond to unseen texts in your specification, undertaking the sort of exercises provided in this workbook will give you confidence and a sense of focus when you come to do so.

It is important to realise that any useful relationship between texts should be a dynamic one. Intertextuality is not about exploring the texts separately in detail and then making some brief comparative points. The demands of this part of the specifications (particularly at A2) place the skill of comparison right at the centre of your work. They are about the many different ways that texts can be compared and contrasted, using both detailed analysis and wider critical perspectives.

The assessment of intertextuality concerns two key aspects:
- developing a confident technique in order to explore and relate unseen and prepared texts
- sharpening the way you use your wider reading to support and develop your responses and ideas

This workbook focuses on developing these two areas.

Making connections: an introduction

The meaning of intertextuality

It is important to remember that no text exists entirely on its own. It is not only critics and readers who make the links; they are already there. In general, there are two ways in which we explore the relationships between texts.

First, we can *focus on a single text*, using other texts to explore and explain where the key text 'came from' (e.g. historical context or other influences) and the writers' relationship with their material (e.g. tone or ideology).

1 Take as many of the texts that you are studying as you can, and write brief notes on how you might explore them through looking at other types of text. Perhaps you could look at other books by the writer or some of his/her contemporaries? Don't develop your ideas in any detail. This is only a preliminary exercise, and you will be expanding on them at a later stage.

....

....

....

....

....

....

....

....

....

....

....

....

....

....

Second, we can *focus on a group of texts*, exploring the meaning and impact of a whole group of texts through developing a range of connections and links between them. Themes might include such subjects as war or marriage.

2 a Take, for example, the theme of division or boundaries, a general area that covers ideas of separateness and isolation. On a large sheet of paper, brainstorm the idea, covering as many possibilities as you can. You might include such aspects of the theme as political division, family issues, gender and ideological divisions.

b Then, in this workbook, write out a list that relates each one of your examples of the theme either to a specific text or a type of text (e.g. an action thriller).

....

....

....

....

....

....

....

....

....

....

....

....

....

....

....

....

....

c Now consider what we might learn from looking at all these connected texts. Note down your ideas. You might, for example, want to make a comment about the way societies have different attitudes and values that divide them (AO5), or the different ways contrasting genres explore the theme (as in Shakespeare's tragedy *Romeo and Juliet* and Brian Friel's play *Translations*).

....

....

....

....

....

....

....

....

....

....

....

(Continued overleaf)

....

Three types of intertextuality

These are:

- connections made by the writer intentionally through *allusion and reference*
- links between a text and other texts that have a direct or indirect *influence* on the writing process
- connections made by *readers*, through their own reading of other texts

We will explore each one of these in turn below. Discuss the three types of connections with other students, using examples from your A-level course, your GCSE reading or your own personal reading. You may want to use the following notes and questions as a basis for your discussion.

Allusions and references

In film, there are a number of examples where particular scenes refer to earlier works by famous directors like Hitchcock. You don't need to pick up on the references to enjoy the film, but they provide another layer of meaning if you do.

It is often the same when reading a novel. If you have read *Frankenstein* (1818), for example, you will know that Mary Shelley refers to Milton's *Paradise Lost*, the Bible and a number of other texts that would have been familiar to readers of the time. She does this primarily to strengthen the central metaphors and themes of the novel, such as creation, families and journeys.

In drama, writers sometimes create a different version of a famous play, as Tom Stoppard did when he thought up the idea of *Rosencrantz and Guildenstern Are Dead* (1967), which is a clever version of Shakespeare's *Hamlet*, focusing on the story of two minor characters in the original play. Again, although you can still enjoy the play without reading *Hamlet*, you will inevitably miss something.

There are also many spoofs and parodies of particular genres, particularly with poetry, but in these cases the connection between the texts is actually the whole point of the exercise.

3 a Think about the different ways in which writers can use other texts to achieve particular effects, often (but not always) for comic purposes. This can include offering contrasts or parallels, or providing a wider understanding in the mind of the reader. Write up your notes.

_____

_____

_____

_____

_____

b Explore the way in which this sort of connection might change your reading experience. Think about how genre influences our expectations and therefore how writers can manipulate our responses by using allusions and references. Again, make sure you have some clear ideas and examples written up below.

_____

_____

_____

_____

_____

_____

_____

Influence

What do we mean by influence? Sometimes writers are well aware of what has influenced them. Occasionally, they even write in direct response to another text. But again, often a work of literature has emerged from a complex web of influences, which could be personal, literary, political or social. Writers can be influenced by particular situations or problems, and these then become the central theme or metaphor of their work. Or, less centrally, they can pick up on a range of smaller literary or social issues or concerns and weld them together to create something new.

Intertextuality can help to place these various potential and actual influences alongside the original text and encourage us to look at the way they might or might not be related.

4 a Take a text that you know or are studying and prepare a diagram on a large sheet of paper that connects it with other texts which may have influenced it. These may be common to the time and genre (like the Bible) or specific to the writer. Try to include as many possible influences as you can, from popular texts the writer may have read to fashionable ideas of the time.

b Now make two lists. In one, indicate which of these connections or relationships are almost certain to have provided an influence, and in the second, list *possible* influences.

Readers

What do we bring to our own reading? Without even thinking, each time we read a book or a poem we instinctively 'place' it by considering it next to those we have read before. We might judge or evaluate it, or simply acknowledge that it is related in some way to other texts. In other words, what we have read (probably since we started to read) is going to have an effect, however small, on each successive text we internalise. This, then, is another sort of intertextuality.

5 a Make a list of the books that you have read which, for whatever reason, you particularly remember, concentrating on imaginative literature rather than non-fiction. You can go as far back in your reading as you like. Discuss your list with others.

b Now consider how your past reading may be influencing the present. For example, do you compare the two, and make judgements on which is better? Do you look back on what you used to read and wonder why you felt like you did about those texts? In this way you can map out your changing reading patterns. Have you recently reread (or seen a film version) of a book you read when you were younger? How did you respond?

(Continued overleaf)

Why compare texts?

Many critics point out that the most interesting point about literature is the differences between texts rather than the similarities. However, when we are asked to explore texts, both are important.

More than anything else, when we compare two or more texts, we need to be clear about why we are bothering to do so. What do we hope to gain or prove? If they are very different in theme or style or genre, we have to be sure that we are going to say something more than just that they are very different.

The following sorts of comparison can produce interesting results:
- exploring two (or more) texts that have a different view or take a different attitude to a similar subject
- exploring two (or more) texts which, although they might have some similarities, use different literary styles and genres to create their impact

Above all, though, such comparisons need a focused approach. Read through these famous poems, which are all about London.

Extract 1

I wander thro' each charter'd street,
Near where the charter'd Thames does flow,
And mark in every face I meet
Marks of weakness, marks of woe.

In every cry of every Man,
In every Infant's cry of fear,
In every voice, in every ban,
The mind-forg'd manacles I hear.

How the Chimney-sweeper's cry
Every black'ning Church appalls;
And the hapless Soldier's sigh
Runs in blood down Palace walls.

But most thro' midnight streets I hear
How the youthful Harlot's curse
Blasts the new-born Infant's tear,
And blights with plagues the Marriage hearse.

William Blake, 'London' from *Songs of Experience* (1791)

Extract 2

Earth has not anything to show more fair:
 Dull would he be of soul who could pass by
 A sight so touching in its majesty:
This City now doth, like a garment, wear
The beauty of the morning; silent, bare,
 Ships, towers, domes, theatres, and temples lie
 Open unto the fields, and to the sky;
All bright and glittering in the smokeless air.
Never did the sun more beautifully steep
 In his first splendour, valley, rock, or hill;
Ne'er saw I, never felt, a calm so deep!
 The river glideth at his own sweet will:
Dear God! the very houses seem asleep;
 And all that mighty heart is lying still!

William Wordsworth, 'Composed upon Westminster Bridge'
(1802)

Extract 3

An omnibus across the bridge
 Crawls like a yellow butterfly,
 And, here and there, a passer-by
Shows like a little restless midge.

Big barges full of yellow hay
 Are moored against the shadowy wharf,
 And, like a yellow silken scarf,
The thick fog hangs along the quay.

The yellow leaves begin to fade
 And flutter from the Temple elms,
 And at my feet the pale green Thames
Lies like a rod of rippled jade.

Oscar Wilde, 'Symphony in Yellow' (1889)

6 a Jot down any basic links between the poems that occur to you (e.g. one is more complex or more personal and one uses more imagery)

....

....

(Continued overleaf)

....

....

....

b Now read the poems again and make a longer, more detailed list of what strikes you as their similarities and differences (e.g. looking in more detail at the structure, the tone and the type of vocabulary).

....

....

....

....

....

....

....

....

....

c Reconsider your list from part b, asking yourself what each one of these similarities and differences actually tells you about the poems. At this stage you are aiming to probe further. Can you say anything about *why* (as well as how) they are the same or different? You need to be more ambitious here, looking for example at how they differ because of their genre, context or ideology.

....

....

....

....

....

....

....

....

Group comparisons

7 It would be best to work in groups of three or four for this activity, although you can, of course, explore the differences and similarities between any group of texts at home. Each member of the group should bring along a poem of reasonable length (about a page or less) that they know but, most importantly, the others don't. The poems can be from any period and about any subject, but ensure that they are all by different writers.

a Start with the text that you have brought along and write down five key things about it. You should try to cover as many of the key areas as possible, for example, subject matter, style, genre and theme.

b Now swap the texts round. This time (without discussing anything with the others) see if you can do the same thing with one of the poems you don't know. Then swap again, until you have seen and commented on each poem.

(Continued overleaf)

c You should now have several lists, which might comment on the writers' attitude to war (or whatever the subject matter is), the form of the poems and the way they use imagery. The aim now is to work together to create a group list of differences and similarities, bringing together all the individual lists.

d Finally, you need to think back over what you have done and answer two questions:
- What can you take away from all this? List what you have learned from the comparisons. Refer to other parts of this introductory section if you are short of ideas.
- Think about how you responded to the texts that you knew compared to those that you didn't. This is important, because some questions in the examinations may ask you to look at unseen material, some that you have prepared and some a mixture of the two.

Developing links beyond comparison

For example, we can:

- Use one (or more) texts to help us understand others by using contextual information (historical, biographical etc).
- Explore the way readers have responded to the different texts by looking at reviews and criticism. What was the focus of their comments? Were they interested in the form and structure or the values and attitudes? Or were they concerned more with the text as a reflection of society and its ideology?
- Explore the way the texts have used different genres, satisfying or denying the readers' expectations.
- Use a range of texts to develop particular critical approaches (such as political speeches for a historicist analysis). Another workbook in this series looks at critical theory.

8 Take one (or more) of the texts you are studying and use these ideas to explore possible connections. For example, research how the text was reviewed when it was first published. Did the reviews relate the text to others (either favourably or not)? What attitude did the reviewer have to the text under review? All of these questions can lead you to explore connections. Make notes on what you learn.

(Continued overleaf)

Using a range of texts

A literary text can be compared to many other types of writing, for example to:

- A so-called 'generic' literary text, in the sense that although it is an imaginative work, it is seen as more of a 'type' than an individual work. Although it may be popular it will not be considered as part of the literary 'club', or the canon as it is called. Popular generic literary texts would include action thrillers, romance and detective stories.
- Non-fiction or factual texts, such as a newspaper articles, letters, journals, biographies and reviews.

The 'generic' text and literature

First, it is worth thinking about how critics (and to some degree all readers) separate 'real' literature from those texts that are considered to be something else (Christmas card greetings, for example). In other words, we are looking at a question which is often asked — what is literature?

Here are some suggestions, but don't presume that everybody agrees. There are no 'right answers' here.

- In 'literature' the language tends to draw attention to itself, to perform or show off (rather than just carry out a simple objective like a manual for a car).
- Although literature does not have to be complicated, it generally has what is called 'density of meaning'. Readers can respond in different ways to a range of possible meanings and ideas, possibly contradictory or ambiguous.
- The significance of a literary text is not limited to one place, one time or one person's experience. It has a general or universal relevance (its importance lasts over time and across the world).
- The form or organisation of the piece is coherent and plays an important part in its overall impact.

9 a What do you think about these statements? Do you want to change or add to them? Finalise your list and then talk about them with others. Make sure you fully understand the meaning of each one.

b Now, taking each statement that you have decided to include in turn, draw up a list of those types of writing that *on this ground alone* you would exclude from the so-called 'literature club', explaining your reasons. For example, contemporary satire doesn't pass the test for being universal because in a short time no reader will be able to understand the point it's making.

....
....
....
....
....
....
....
....
....
....

c Now draw up another list, which pairs off what you consider to be a literary text against one that for whatever reason 'fails the test'. For example, a passionate scene from a recognised 'classic' like *Wuthering* Heights or *Jane Eyre* and a scene from a Mills and Boon romantic novel. Write notes about what we can learn about *both* texts in each pairing that you make. Are there similarities as well as differences?

....
....
....
....
....
....

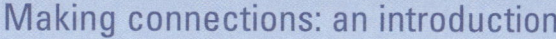

Connecting a range of different types of text

The texts that follow are divided into two small groups. The first is based around the general theme of spying, and the second is a cluster of extracts and texts related to Emily Brontë's novel *Wuthering Heights*.

There are a range of different styles and genres here, and part of this activity is to explore and comment on the writing itself (assessed in AO3). In addition, however, you are going to consider the potential relationships that may exist between the texts.

Spying and spies

For various reasons, spying has become a literary and media obsession since the Second World War. These brief extracts include passages from two well-known novels, a poem and a work of non-fiction. They explore different aspects of what it is to be a spy or terrorist, and provide some discussion of the implications of spying.

Extract 1

Control of the passes was, he saw, the key
To this new district, but who would get it?
He, the trained spy, had walked into the trap
For a bogus guide, seduced with the old tricks.
At Greenhearth was a fine site for a dam
And easy power, had they pushed the rail
Some stations nearer. They ignored his wires.
The bridges were unbuilt and trouble coming.
The street music seemed gracious now to one
For weeks up in the desert. Woken by water
Running away in the dark, he often had
Reproached the night for a companion
Dreamed of already. They would shoot of course,
Parting easily who were never joined.

W. H. Auden, 'The Secret Agent' (1928) from *Collected Poems*
(Faber and Faber Ltd)

Extract 2

At least we have large and able security organizations to protect us from our spies; and it is impossible not to applaud the courageous and shrewd and patient men who work to preserve our national safety. Yet they too are a source of danger to the State. The essential conditions of their being work out badly for themselves and everybody else. They can only find the infinitesimally small proportion of populations which take to spying by subjecting large numbers of persons to restrictions on their freedom which it is a good citizen's duty to protest against, unless he is told the reason for them, which is often inadvisable from a security point of view. The officers are obliged to work in the strictest secrecy, and this is unhealthy.

Rebecca West, *The Meaning of Treason* (1949)

Extract 3

Verloc, an anarchist — at least in theory — and the main character in the novel is being lectured to by Mr Vladimir, his spymaster, about the need for some major incident.

This is what you should try for. An attempt upon a crowned head or on a president is sensational enough in a way, but not so much as it used to be. It has entered into the general conception of the existence of all chiefs of state. It's almost conventional — especially since so many presidents have been assassinated. Now let us take an outrage upon — say, a church. Horrible enough at first sight, no doubt, and yet not so effective as a person of an ordinary mind might think. No matter how revolutionary and anarchist in inception, there would be fools enough to give such an outrage the character of a religious manifestation. And that would detract from the especial alarming significance we wish to give to the act. A murderous attempt on a restaurant or a theatre would suffer in the same way from the suggestion of non-political passion; the exasperation of a hungry man, an act of social revenge. All this is used up; it is no longer instructive as an object lesson in revolutionary anarchism. Every newspaper has ready-made phrases to explain such manifestations away. ...A bomb outrage to have any influence on public opinion now must go beyond the intention of vengeance or terrorism. It must be purely destructive. It must be that, and only that, beyond the faintest suspicion of any other object. You anarchists should make it clear that you are perfectly determined to make a clean sweep of the whole social creation. But how to get that appallingly absurd notion into the heads of the middle classes so that there should be no mistake? That's the question. By directing your blows at something outside the ordinary passions of humanity is the answer. ... They believe that in some mysterious way science is at the source of their material prosperity. They do. And the absurd ferocity of such a demonstration will affect them more profoundly than the mangling of a whole street — or theatre — full of their own kind. ...The demonstration must be against learning — science. But not every science will do. The attack must have all the shocking senselessness of gratuitous blasphemy.

Joseph Conrad, *The Secret Agent* (1907)

Extract 4

In Leamas, the main character in the novel, John le Carré paints a forceful picture of an isolated spy working among the uncertainties of the Cold War.

A man who lives a part, not to others but alone, is exposed to obvious psychological dangers. In itself, the practice of deception is not particularly exacting; it is a matter of experience, of professional expertise, it is a facility most of us can acquire. But while a confidence trickster, a play-actor or a gambler can return from his performance to the ranks of his admirers, the secret agent enjoys no such relief. For him, deception is first a matter of self-defence. He must protect himself not only from without but from within, and against the most natural of impulses; though he earn a fortune, his role may forbid him the purchase of a razor, though he be erudite, it can befall him to mumble nothing but banalities; though he be an affectionate husband and father, he must under all circumstances withhold himself from those in whom he should naturally confide.

Aware of the overwhelming temptations which assail a man permanently isolated in his deceit, Leamas resorted to the course which armed him best; even when he was alone, he compelled himself to live with the personality he had assumed.

John le Carré, *The Spy who Came in from the Cold* (1963)

10 Using different pairings of these texts, explore the way spies and spying are presented here. Refer carefully to the genre in each case.

....

....

....

....

....

....

....

....

....

....

....

....

....

....

....

....

....

(Continued overleaf)

....

....

....

....

....

Wuthering Heights

Emily Brontë's novel *Wuthering Heights* (1847) is one of the most famous and best loved of all nineteenth-century novels. The story concerns the conflicts and tensions between two families, with a central narrative that focuses on a passionate but doomed love affair and the tortured lives of almost all the central characters. Although the novel is influenced by the tradition of the Gothic novel, it is a much more complex and challenging text than that implies, with an intricate narrative structure that encompasses a range of points of view. The novel was published under the name of Ellis Bell.

The first three extracts are from contemporary reviewers.

Extract 1

What may be the moral which the author wishes the reader to deduce from the work it is difficult to say, and we refrain from assigning any, because, to speak honestly, we have discovered none but mere glimpses of hidden morals or secondary meanings. There seems to us great power in this book, but a purposeless power, which we feel a great desire turned to better account.

From a review in Douglas Jerrold's *Weekly Newspaper* (15 January 1848)

Extract 2

In spite of much power and cleverness; in spite of its truth to life in the remote nooks and corners of England *Wuthering Heights* is a disagreeable story.

From a review in *Athenaeum* (December 1847)

Extract 3

The story shows the brutalising influence of unchecked passion. His characters are a commentary on the truth that there is no tyranny in the world like that which thoughts of evil exercise in the daring and reckless breast.

From a review in *Britannia* (January 1848)

Extract 4

Emily Brontë's sister Charlotte describes the creation of the novel in a famous passage:

> *Wuthering Heights* was hewn in a wild workshop, with simple tools, out of homely materials. The statuary [sculptor] found a granite block on a solitary moor: gazing thereon, he saw how from the crag might be elicited a head [...] With time and labour, the crag took human shape; and there it stands colossal, dark and frowning, half statue, half rock.
>
> From Charlotte Brontë's preface to the 1850 edition of *Wuthering Heights*

11 a Explore what Emily Brontë's contemporary critics were saying about the novel through a close analysis of some of the key words and phrases. What attitudes and values can you detect in their comments?

....

....

....

....

....

....

....

....

....

....

....

b Research some recent criticism of *Wuthering Heights* and compare not only what the critics are saying about the novel but the language that they use. In what ways are the aims and methods of literary criticism different now? Write notes on your research.

....

....

....

....

(Continued overleaf)

c What do you learn from Charlotte Brontë's words about her attitude to the novel?

12 a Summarise any useful links you can make between the two groups of passages.

b Finally, think about what you might do to research these connections further.

....

....

....

....

....

....

....

Film and literature

We are used to referring to films as 'texts' and they certainly provide another possible type of link and connection. Despite what the film director Ingmar Bergman said — 'Film has nothing to do with literature' — there are a number of ways in which creating connections between the two can help us explore texts. Perhaps the two most obvious areas for the development of connections are the many different versions of Shakespeare's plays and adaptations of novels (both contemporary and 'classic') on film or television. Many people feel that famous novels, like those of Jane Austen, somehow 'belong' to us and respond angrily to adaptations that they consider fail to support their interpretation of these novels. Nevertheless, film versions of classic fiction are always popular and can introduce the text to a wider audience.

How can making links with films help us understand texts?

- The ways in which films are structured can sometimes help us to understand how, for example, Shakespeare and his contemporaries developed their fast flowing dramatic action that has, in fact, often been called 'filmic'.
- The way in which films tell the story can be a useful point of comparison: point of view, narrative sequences, contrasts etc.
- The economical and focused way films convey information can be compared to fiction.
- The effective way films create visual statements through the use of focused detail can be compared to the use of imagery in fiction.
- Adaptations of texts can often help us to see the original in a new light, and encourage us to see a wider range of interpretations.

On the other hand, there are some who consider that, just as literature is emphasising the role of the reader as part of an interactive and creative relationship with the text, film (with its sense of visual 'completeness') denies the viewer that freedom.

13 a In a group, go through the points on p. 25 and discuss in broad terms the ways in which films and novels differ. Make careful notes.

b Discuss the images or sequences that you best remember from films you have seen. Why do they stick in your memory?

c Think about film or television adaptations of a novel or play that you are familiar with. Make a list of five ways in which the adaptations added to or departed from the original. Which were most successful, and why?

d Develop two lists of films. One is a list of films that are close to literature, i.e. they tell their story in a similar way. For example, although some novels use flashback techniques, most tell a sequential story. Most twentieth-century plays limit the place and time in order to focus the narrative action. The other list should be of films which are obviously more filmic, i.e. they do not tell a 'traditional' story, but perhaps create their effect through symbolism or a series of apparently unconnected narratives.

How to explore a range of connections

14 Choose **one** of the texts that you are studying as the basis for this exercise. Try to focus on one that you have not used in the other activities. Start by going back to the preliminary list you made for Question 1 at the beginning of this section.

Briefly remind yourself of the various ways that we can make connections between texts that we explored in the introductory section. Establish as many connections with your chosen text as you can.

Do some carefully focused research so that you can be more specific about the connections that you want to make.

At the end of your work, write a brief analysis of what all these connections have taught you about your text.

A suggested study programme:

- Choose your text (prose, poetry or drama) and ask yourself if there is another text by the same writer with which it would be useful to make an extended comparison.
- Explore other useful texts by the same writer (perhaps non-literary texts such as letters).
- Now place the text in its period by considering other contemporary texts — literary and non-literary.
- Explore its genre by considering other texts of a similar genre (both contemporary and from other periods).
- Finally, identify the key theme and relate it to other texts.

Bringing together the Assessment Objectives

A reminder of how intertextuality can help you focus on the key objectives:
- the way a particular genre has developed over time
- the influence of particular contextual factors
- the way style/language/structure changes according to genre, period, tone and literary aim and intention
- the ideological basis of the writing — the way the author has approached the subject matter or theme

Some questions to ask about texts

Following on from the reminder above about the importance of the assessment objectives, and to finish this introductory section, here is a list of some useful questions to ask when responding to a group of potentially interlinked texts:
- Are any of the texts written by the same person? If so, is there any biographical information that it would be useful to know?
- Are they written by different people but in the same period? If so, are there important contextual factors that might have influenced them?
- Although they may have been written at roughly the same time, are there *generic* issues which mean that they take a different approach to the subject matter?
- If the texts are written in different time periods, how does this affect the way they approach the subject matter (such as their attitudes and values)?

'Placing' a text

What does 'placing' mean?

In some ways, it means 'contextualising' — placing the key text next to other texts in order to explore its source, meaning, genre and relationship with sociopolitical, philosophical or cultural issues. The requirement to provide context for most of the texts that you study is closely related to this aspect of intertextuality.

However, what we are focusing on here is the way that we can 'place' texts in this way, not through researching information (about the politics of the time or the writer's biography, for example), but through other texts (in this case, literary). This also involves research, but rather than compiling information, you need to find other texts that will clarify your key text(s).

If you were studying *1984* (1949) by George Orwell, you might wish to relate it to:
- *Animal Farm* (1945), another text by Orwell, which explores in the form of a fable what happens when an idealistic communist state turns into a dictatorship
- *The Handmaid's Tale* (1985) by Margaret Atwood, in which women in particular are subjected to the horrifying demands of a totalitarian state
- Ray Bradbury's *Fahrenheit 451* (1953), which imagines a world in which all books are burned as being subversive
- Aldous Huxley's novel *Brave New World* (1932), in which everybody is 'forced' to be happy
- *Children of Men* (1996), a novel by P. D. James, which narrates what happens when all the women in the world become sterile

1 On a large sheet of paper, develop a diagram with your main text, for example *1984*, in the centre and related texts around it. Each relationship should be labelled. For example, a particular text that you are relating to the main one could be similar in genre but perhaps different in subject matter, and this should be made clear.

List below what you have gained from this exercise — how has the text been 'placed'?

Developing an interpretation

Interpretations are the most creative way to approach a text, and the way to satisfy the demands of AO4 (your response and that of others) and AO3 (detailed analysis of the text). They are the result of you — the reader — interacting with what you are reading and developing a view, an attitude, an understanding. It is not about evaluating how 'good' the text is, but about the way you make your own sense of the text.

How can intertextuality help that process?

If we imagine that interpretations are a combination of making clear, personal decisions and then exploring and testing them against the text, then intertextuality allows you to make statements about the type of text (genre) or the relationship between the subject matter and the writer (tone), then to test them against a range of other texts.

1 Take one of the texts you are studying and do the following:

a Write down five clear statements about the text, each of which covers a different aspect, for example, character or language. Make sure they are interpretations not just descriptions — not what is agreed by all to be in the text but what *you* think is important and interesting.

....

....

....

....

....

....

....

b Find out any useful statements that the writer made, not necessarily about the text you are studying, but perhaps about other works of literature, or anything else that appears relevant.

....

....

....

....

....

....

....

c Research any contemporary reviews of the text.

d Explore what the critics have written about it.

e Finally, go back to your original interpretations and write five paragraphs (one for each interpretation) incorporating as much of the information as you can, but not losing sight of your own ideas. Refer clearly to the different texts, using direct quotation where possible.

Periods and themes

Making connections through themes but across different time periods is probably the most useful (and possibly the easiest) way to explore intertextuality. Among other things it should provide you with some clear material for context (AO5).

Consider the theme of adultery, for example. Adultery is a popular literary subject for a number of reasons:

- It can be developed to suit different genres (comedy, farce, tragedy).
- It is a useful theme for the development of character.
- It is likely to include certain key aspects of many narratives, such as secrets, conflict and passion.
- It can be used effectively to explore social attitudes and values.

As far as developing connections is concerned, the idea of adultery can lead to interesting generic comparisons, explorations of different social structures and religious and moral codes. For example, the act of adultery can be seen in some social and literary contexts as an act of freedom — an expression of individual liberty. In other cases, adultery can be viewed as a powerful statement, a rejection of the married state itself (an action either criticised or supported). It can centre on a whole range of gender issues and on attitudes to marriage.

Another way in which we can make connections between different representations of adultery is through exploring tone and style. Tone, broadly speaking, is the attitude that writers adopt towards their subject matter — for example, angry or celebratory — and style is the writer's choice of vocabulary and the structure and form they adopt (as assessed in AO3). These choices of style can, in turn, be seen to reflect the tone.

As an example, we can look at the comedy of manners, a genre that has been popular in drama and fiction for many centuries, such as in some of Shakespeare's comedies, in seventeenth-century Restoration comedy, in eighteenth-century sentimental comedy and in the plays of Oscar Wilde (1890s). This genre focuses on the behaviour of social groups or individuals and invites us to laugh at them. The degree to which this laughter is cruel or more forgiving depends on the tone adopted by the writer. Since the most popular plot for many of these plays is centred on adultery (actual or merely hinted at, laughed at or admired), this genre is particularly useful for exploring how tone and style can affect our response to adulterous behaviour.

In Restoration comedy, young, attractive and amusing men are often presented favourably through their use of language, and this protects them from our disapproval. By providing such characters with witty remarks, the writer establishes a particular 'tone' that sends out the signal that what they get up to is acceptable, and even admirable.

1 Work in a small group for this activity but use your workbook to keep track of your ideas. Each member of the group needs to think of two themes that could be explored effectively across different periods (in other words, don't choose an idea that is too time-specific). Possible areas include war, marriage, work and death. Then, research your two ideas and come up with some texts that are related through the theme. At this stage, they can be specific texts or vaguer, more generic ideas. Talk in the group about your ideas, identifying in each case, a way in which you could connect them, and how the different periods have affected the writing.

Concentrate on **one** theme only and plan out the connections that you think it would be useful to make. Use headings such as genre, subject matter, tone, context and style, and develop a clear idea of why each link might be useful.

Write up all your notes so that you have a clear presentation and, if you can, copy it and exchange your ideas with other groups. Your work should cover:

- a range of texts connected by theme but written at different times
- a clear explanation of why this is a useful exercise — what have you learned?

Of course, connections to the theme of adultery are not restricted to printed fiction. Here are a few from drama, and there are also possibilities from film and television.

- Chaucer's *The Merchant's Tale* explores traditional territory through the adulterous triangle of the old but rich husband, the young, attractive wife and the young lover. The meaning of the tale is clearly weighted on the side of youth.
- There are surprisingly few references to adultery in Shakespeare. Two plays — *The Winter's Tale* and *Othello* — are, however, about sexual jealousy and the way it can destroy and fracture an apparently settled existence.
- Restoration comedies (written after 1660) are nearly all about adultery in one form or another. For example, William Wycherley's play *The Country Wife* (1675) is based on a trick that the main character, Horner, plays on married men to enable him to seduce their wives.
- As divorce has become easier and more common in recent times and the inhibitions that used to surround the subject of sexual behaviour on stage have largely disappeared, the way in which adultery is given dramatic life has changed. You might want to explore some examples of recent television drama, films or plays that take adultery as a theme. One example is Harold Pinter's play *Betrayal* (1983), which recounts the story of an adulterous affair — backwards.

2 What type of connections to drama, television and film could you make for your chosen theme?

The third day, in the morning, the wind having abated overnight, the sea was calm, and I ventur'd; but I am a warning to all rash and ignorant pilots; for no sooner was I come to the point, when I was not even my boat's length from the shore, but I found myself in a great depth of water, and a current like the sluice of a mill: it carried my boat along with it with such violence that all I could do could not keep her so much as on the edge of it; but I found it hurry'd me farther and farther out from the eddy, which was on my left hand. There was no wind stirring to help me, and all I could do with my paddlers signify'd nothing, and now I began to give myself over for lost; for as the current was on both sides of the island, I knew in a few leagues' distance they must join again, and then I was irrecoverably gone; nor did I see any possibility of avoiding it; so that I had no prospect before me but of perishing, not by the sea, for that was calm enough, but of starving from hunger. I had, indeed, found a tortoise on the shore, as big almost as I could lift, and had toss'd it into the boat; and I had a great jar of fresh water, that is to say, one of my earthen pots; but what was all this to being driven into the vast ocean, where, to be sure, there was no shore, no mainland or island, for a thousand leagues at least?

And now I saw how easy it was for the providence of God to make even the most miserable condition mankind could be in, worse. Now I look'd back upon my desolate, solitary island as the most pleasant place in the world, and all the happiness my heart could wish for was to be but there again.

1 Write some careful notes on this extract. Focus on two particular aspects:
- Crusoe's responses to the world around him
- the ways in which you respond to him

Now, read these much shorter examples of travel writing, which describe the writers' experiences of different places.

Extract 2

Awakening early on that first morning, I slipped on a dressing gown provided by the hotel and went out on the veranda. In the dawn light the sky was a pale grey-blue and, after the rustlings of the night before, all the creatures and even the wind seemed in deep sleep. It was as quiet as a library. Beyond the hotel room stretched a wide beach which was covered at first with coconut trees and then sloped unhindered towards the sea. I climbed over the veranda's low railing and walked across the sand. Nature was at her most benevolent. It was as if, in creating this small horseshoe bay, she had chosen to atone for her ill-temper in other regions and decided for once to display only her munificence. The trees provided shade and milk, the floor of the sea was lined with shells, the sand was powdery and the colour of sun-ripened wheat, and the air — even in the shade — had an enveloping, profound warmth to it so unlike the fragility of northern European heat, always prone to cede, even in midsummer, to a more assertive, proprietary chill.

Alain de Botton, *The Art of Travel* (2002)

Extract 3

Cold, fresh wind, a black-blue, translucent, rolling sea on which the waves rose in snapping foam, and Sicily on the left: Monte Pellegrino, a huge, inordinate mass of pinkish rock, hardly crisped with the faintest vegetation, looming up to heaven from the sea. Strangely large in mass and bulk Monte Pellegrino looks: and bare, like a Sahara in heaven: and old-looking. These coasts of Sicily are very imposing, terrific, fortifying the interior. And again one gets the feeling that age has worn them bare: as if old, old civilizations had worn away and exhausted the soil, leaving a terrifying blankness of rock.

D. H. Lawrence, *Sea and Sardinia* (1923)

Extract 4

Spain is one of the absolutes. Most states nowadays are willy-nilly passive, subject always to successive alien forces. Spain still declines in the active mood. She is not a Great Power, but in her minor way she is one of the prime movers still — still a nation that sets its own standards. To us poor ciphers of the computer culture, us cosmopolitan, humanist, cynical serfs of the machine, nothing is more compelling than the drama, at once dark and dazzling, of that theatre over the hills — the vast splendour of the Spanish landscape, the intensity of Spain's pride and misery, the adventurous glory of a history that set its seal upon half the world, the sadness of a decline that edged so inexorably from triumph to tragedy, through so many centuries of rot. All this, distilled in blazing heat and venomous cold, dusted by the sand of Africa, guarded by that mountain barricade above you — all this seems to await your arrival, beyond the pass of Roncesvalles.

Jan Morris, *Spain* (1964)

Extract 5

In the small hours that night, when I looked out of my porthole again, I found we were sailing through an endless parade of ships, gloomily illuminated in the darkness: and when at crack of dawn I went on deck to a drizzly morning, still we were passing them, up a scummy river now, lined with ships, thick with ships, barges and tugs, and container ships, and a warship or two, and country craft of shambled wood so fibrous and stringy-looking that it seemed to me the Chinese, who eat anything, might well make a dish of them. Hooting all the way we edged a passage up the Huangpu, narrowly avoiding ferry-boats, sending sampans scurrying for safety, until after thirty miles of ships, and docks, and grimy warehouses, and factories, we saw before us a waterfront façade of high towers and office buildings, red and shabby in the rain. It was my China landfall: it was the city of Shanghai.

Jan Morris, *A Writer's World* (2003)

2 a Write notes on how these writers attempt to explore the meaning and significance of their environment.

....

....

....

....

....

....

....

....

b What do your notes tell you about the genre of travel writing as represented here by these passages? Think particularly about the readers' expectations.

....

....

....

....

....

....

....

....

....

c Think about the differences (if any) between the way these writers are describing place and the way a novelist would.

....

....

....

....

....

....

....

....

....

Read carefully the verses that follow. The first is an extract from Byron's long poem *Childe Harold's Pilgrimage*, a romantic description of travels across Europe, particularly Greece and Italy. This extract is from the end of Canto 4, which was published in 1818. It is an impassioned response to the power of nature, in general, and the sea in particular.

Extract 6

> Oh! that the Desart were my dwelling-place,
> With one fair Spirit for my minister,
> That I might all forget the human race,
> And, hating no one, love but only her!
> Ye Elements!—in whose enobling stir
> I feel myself exalted—Can ye not
> Accord me such a being? Do I err
> In deeming such inhabit many a spot?
> Though with them to converse can rarely be our lot.
>
> There is a pleasure in the pathless woods,
> There is a rapture on the lonely shore,
> There is society, where none intrudes,
> By the deep Sea, and music in its roar;
> I love not Man the less, but Nature more,
> From these our interviews, in which I steal
> From all I may be, or have been before,
> To mingle with the Universe, and feel
> What I can ne'er express, yet cannot all conceal.

> Roll on, thou deep and dark blue Ocean—roll!
> Ten thousand fleets sweep over thee in vain;
> Man marks the earth with ruin—his control
> Stops with the shore; upon the watery plain
> The wrecks are all thy deed, nor doth remain
> A shadow of man's ravage, save his own,
> When, for a moment, like a drop of rain,
> He sinks into thy depths with bubbling groan,
> Without a grave, unknell'd, uncoffin'd, and unknown.

The next extract is taken from Wordsworth's poem 'Lines Composed a Few Miles above Tintern Abbey' (1798), which he wrote on returning to Tintern five years after his original visit.

Extract 7

> Five years have past; five summers, with the length
> Of five long winters! and again I hear
> These waters, rolling from their mountain-springs
> With a soft inland murmur.—Once again
> Do I behold these steep and lofty cliffs,
> That on a wild secluded scene impress
> Thoughts of more deep seclusion; and connect
> The landscape with the quiet of the sky.
> The day is come when I again repose
> Here, under this dark sycamore, and view
> These plots of cottage-ground, these orchard-tufts,
> Which at this season, with their unripe fruits,
> Are clad in one green hue, and lose themselves
> 'Mid groves and copses. Once again I see
> These hedge-rows, hardly hedge-rows, little lines
> Of sportive wood run wild: these pastoral farms,
> Green to the very door; and wreaths of smoke
> Sent up, in silence, from among the trees!
> With some uncertain notice, as might seem
> Of vagrant dwellers in the houseless woods,
> Or of some Hermit's cave, where by his fire
> The Hermit sits alone.
>   These beauteous forms,
> Through a long absence, have not been to me
> As is a landscape to a blind man's eye:
> But oft, in lonely rooms, and 'mid the din
> Of towns and cities, I have owed to them
> In hours of weariness, sensations sweet,
> Felt in the blood, and felt along the heart;
> And passing even into my purer mind,

With tranquil restoration:—feelings too
Of unremembered pleasure: such, perhaps,
As have no slight or trivial influence
On that best portion of a good man's life,
His little, nameless, unremembered, acts
Of kindness and of love. Nor less, I trust,
To them I may have owed another gift,
Of aspect more sublime; that blessed mood,
In which the burthen of the mystery,
In which the heavy and the weary weight
Of all this unintelligible world,
Is lightened:—that serene and blessed mood,
In which the affections gently lead us on,—
Until, the breath of this corporeal frame
And even the motion of our human blood
Almost suspended, we are laid asleep
In body, and become a living soul:
While with an eye made quiet by the power
Of harmony, and the deep power of joy,
We see into the life of things.

3 In these poems the writers are responding with passion and intensity to the world they see around them. In the case of Byron, he is writing about nature in general; with Wordsworth it is the very particularity of his description that provides the power. Write notes on how these two writers responded to nature.

....

....

....

....

....

....

4 Now consider these wider questions and make notes on your responses.

a Think about the different ways texts can evoke a sense of place. You might consider such aspects as the way details are used to build up a picture in our mind, the power of a strong individual voice and the writers' response to the perceived power of nature.

....

....

....

....

....

....

....

....

....

....

....

....

....

....

....

....

b Explore the different ways in which writers have chosen to represent place over time. You might wish to start by returning to the Defoe, Byron and Wordsworth passages and begin by linking the two extracts from the Romantic poets (what they have in common) and comparing them with the Defoe (how this extract is different). Try to ignore the obvious differences between form and genre (fiction and poetry) and focus on how the narrator or poetic voice relates to the presence of the physical environment.

Grouping texts

Every reader responds differently to the texts that they read, and will read each type of text in a different way. Modern critics often refer to the reader as being part author of a text in this way. In other words, even if we never write a word we can consider the *way* we read as being almost a creative act.

Intertextuality asks us to be creative in our response to linked texts and to bring our own ideas to each pairing or group.

The four extracts and texts that follow are wide-ranging in terms of subject matter, theme, period and genre.

Extract 1

The outskirt of the garden in which Tess found herself had been left uncultivated for some years, and was now damp and rank with juicy grass which sent up mists of pollen at a touch; and with tall blooming weeds emitting offensive smells — weeds whose red and yellow and purple hues formed a polychrome as dazzling as that of cultivated flowers. She went stealthily as a cat through this profusion of growth, gathering cuckoo-spittle on her skirts, cracking snails that were underfoot, staining her hands with thistle-milk and slug-slime, and rubbing off upon her naked arms sticky blights which, though snow-white on the apple-tree trunks, made blood-red stains on her skin; thus she drew quite near to Clare, still unobserved of him.

Tess was conscious of neither time nor space. The exaltation which she had described as being producible at will by gazing at a star, came now without any determination of hers; she undulated upon the thin notes as upon billows, and their harmonies passed like breezes through her, bringing tears into her eyes. The floating pollen seemed to be his notes made visible, and the dampness of the garden the weeping of the garden's sensibility. Though near nightfall, the rank-smelling weed-flowers glowed as if they would not close for intentness, and the waves of colour mixed with the waves of sound.

The light which still shone was derived mainly from a large hole in the western bank of cloud; it was like a piece of day left behind by accident, dusk having closed in elsewhere. He concluded his plaintive melody, a very simple performance, demanding no great skill; and she waited, thinking another might be begun. But, tired of playing, he had desultorily come round the fence, and was rambling up behind her. Tess, her cheeks on fire, moved away furtively, as if hardly moving at all.

Thomas Hardy, *Tess of the d'Urbervilles* (1891)

Extract 2

As a white stone draws down the fish
She on the seafloor of the afternoon
Draws down men's glances and their cruel wish
For love. Her red lip on the spoon
Slips-in a morsel of ice-cream. Her hands
White as a shell, are submarine
Fronds, sink with spread fingers, lean
Along the table, carmined at the ends.
A cotton magnate, an important fish

With great eyepouches and a golden mouth
Through the frail reefs of furniture swims out
And idling, suspended stays to watch.
A crustacean old man clamped to his chair
Sits near her and might coldly see
Her charms through fissures where the eyes should be;
Or else his teeth are parted in a stare.
Captain on leave, a lean dark mackerel,
Lies in the offing, turns himself and looks
Through currents of sound. The flat-eyed flatfish sucks
On a straw, staring from its repose, laxly.
And gallants in shoals swim up and lag,
Circling and passing near the white attraction —
Sometimes pausing, opening a conversation —
Fish pause so to nibble or tug.
But now the ice-cream is finished, is
paid for. The fish swim off on business
And she sits alone at the table, a white stone
Useless except to a collector, a rich man.

Keith Douglas, 'Behaviour of fish in an Egyptian tea garden'

Extract 3

He was working on the edge of the common, beyond the small brook that ran in the dip at the bottom of the garden, carrying the garden path in continuation from the plank bridge on to the common. He had cut the rough turf and bracken, leaving the grey, dryish soil bare. But he was worried because he could not get the path straight, there was a pleat between his brows. He had set up his sticks, and taken the sights between the big pine trees, but for some reason everything seemed wrong. He looked again, straining his keen blue eyes, that had a touch of the Viking in them, through the shadowy pine trees as through a doorway, at the green-grassed garden-path rising from the shadow of alders by the log bridge up to the sunlit flowers. Tall white and purple columbines, and the butt-end of the old Hampshire cottage that crouched near the earth amid flowers, blossoming in the bit of shaggy wildness round about.

D. H. Lawrence, *England, My England* (1924)

Extract 4

WHEN the Present has latched its postern behind my tremulous stay,
    And the May month flaps its glad green leaves like wings,
Delicate-filmed as new-spun silk, will the neighbours say,
    "He was a man who used to notice such things"?

If it be in the dusk when, like an eyelid's soundless blink,
    The dewfall-hawk comes crossing the shades to alight
Upon the wind-warped upland thorn, a gazer may think,
    "To him this must have been a familiar sight."

If I pass during some nocturnal blackness, mothy and warm,
    When the hedgehog travels furtively over the lawn,
One may say, "He strove that such innocent creatures should come to no harm,
    But he could do little for them; and now he is gone."

If, when hearing that I have been stilled at last, they stand at the door,
    Watching the full-starred heavens that winter sees,
Will this thought rise on those who will meet my face no more,
    "He was one who had an eye for such mysteries"?

And will any say when my bell of quittance is heard in the gloom,
    And a crossing breeze cuts a pause in its out-rollings,
Till they rise again, as they were a new bell's boom,
    "He hears it not now, but used to notice such things"?

Thomas Hardy, 'Afterwards' (1917)

1 a Choose two of these texts that you think have enough in common for it to be interesting to explore the similarities (e.g. in style and approach). Write some notes about them as a pair. Remember, not everything has to be the same, just enough for you to explore them. Don't just consider theme — think also about style and form, genre, tone and context. You need to ask yourself whether, for example, it would be more useful to compare two texts by the same author (Thomas Hardy) or not.

(Continued overleaf)

....

....

....

....

....

....

....

....

....

....

....

....

b Keep the same pair and consider what other texts you could add in order to explore the points you have made in more detail.

....

....

....

Coursework

All coursework at this level should involve you in doing some research — taking a topic and exploring it on your own (with some guidelines, of course). There are various types of research:
- you can research contextual information (AO5)
- you can explore the critical context of the text (AO4)
- you can read other texts written by the same author

All of these will require you to make connections of different types:
- between non-literary texts and aspects of the text
- between different critical interpretations of the text and the text itself
- between a range of references from the writer, including letters and diaries

The specifications

The whole point about coursework is that you should be given as much freedom as possible in your choice of text and question, although it may prove more effective for the teacher to agree on one text for the class and propose a set of questions from which you can choose. There are two things to bear in mind,which might in some ways conflict with each other:
- The setting of questions and the choice of text are important decisions and your teacher will want to make sure that you are on the right lines in both decisions. Every year students lose marks in their coursework because they fail to ask the right question, i.e. one that will satisfy the assessment objectives of the unit.
- On the other hand, you need to be happy with the text and topic you are focusing on. So, make sure that when you come to undertake your coursework, you fully understand the text(s) and the implications of your question.

AS specifications

Depending upon the awarding body, the AS specification might require you to do the following in your coursework:
- respond to one text (your own choice) in two different essays — a detailed analysis and an exploration of the whole text
- write about a Shakespeare play chosen from a list or a free choice

The AS specifications do not directly assess your ability to make connections between texts, but when looking at any text you will inevitably do so as part of your research.

A2 specifications

A2 requires you to show that you can make connections. For example, in coursework:
- You might be asked to write about a post-1900 prose text, and although comparison is not a requirement, some candidates choose to write about more than one text when this is an optional element within the unit requirement. Context (AO5) is still assessed, as are critical responses (AO4), and both of these will inevitably provide opportunities for connections.

- You could be asked to respond to a specific part of the examination that focuses on literary connections, through theme, genre or context. In this type of unit, the comparison might also involve critical concepts and an exploration of critical responses to the text.

Using critical texts in coursework

- As with all connections, be absolutely clear why you are making them. What will your essay gain from this?
- Are these links a part of the assessment of the unit? Even if they are not, is it a useful thing to do? Why?
- To what degree are these critical texts a part of your preparation (research, thinking through what you want to say, exploring a range of ideas)?
- Or are they an element that you want to be clearly present in your final essay? In other words, texts that you will refer to and quote.

An example of intertextual coursework

For the purposes of this example, the two texts being studied are both British contemporary novels: Kazuo Ishiguro's *The Remains of the Day* (1989) and Ian McEwan's *Enduring Love* (1997).

Here is a choice of coursework titles.

'Modern fiction often explores the ways in which the ordered and apparently secure lives of the characters collapse under both internal and external pressure.'
To what extent do you agree or disagree with this statement?

'It is the presentation of an obsessed and untrustworthy narrator that provides the drive of the two novels.'
To what extent do you agree or disagree with this statement?

'In both novels the central characters are emotional failures who are unable to make connections with anybody else.'
To what extent do you agree or disagree with this statement?

'Both novels are concerned with the relationship between storytelling and the search for truth.'
To what extent do you agree or disagree with this statement?

Look at the statements in the titles carefully. They were all used as a way to create links between these two contemporary novels. It doesn't matter if you haven't read the novels — just look at the wording of the questions.

1 a Pick out the most important words in each title.

b Consider what each coursework title is asking about. For example, is it focusing on character, narrative technique, theme etc?

c What sort of links could you make between two contemporary novels? For example, the way the story is narrated, point of view etc.

....

....

....

....

....

....

....

....

....

....

d Think about any two contemporary texts that you have read that you could link up in this way. They need to have some clear points of contact (e.g. both focus on the same theme, both about particular problems, both have a similar narrative style). Working with someone else if you prefer, see if you can come up with some coursework titles that link the two texts.

....

....

....

....

....

....

(Continued overleaf)

....

Preparing for examinations

As you have learned throughout this workbook, there are two ways in which intertextuality is important in the A-level literature course:
- First, the A2 specifications require you to link texts.
- Second, even when this is not the case, or when studying for AS, the ability to link and place texts in the ways in which we have discussed is an important skill.

In the A-level examinations, there are several ways in which you might be asked to make connections. The main ones are:
- to write about several texts (usually poetry) written by the same person, in response to a particular question
- to write about several texts (usually poetry) written by different writers, which appear in an anthology, in response to a particular question
- to explore several texts by different writers that are linked through theme, subject matter or genre
- to use one or more texts to develop your understanding of a single key text
- to explore a range of texts of varied genres to develop an overview of a particular subject or theme

Here are some examples of different types of questions involving intertextuality. You must be careful to check your own specification to see where this idea of comparison or connecting is particularly important, and to check the specific wording of the questions in the examination that you will be taking.
- You can be asked to explore a theme in relation to a particular period:
  Discuss the different ways in which writers have explored fear and endurance in their writing about the First World War.
- You could also be asked to compare two texts from a particular point of view:
  Through a comparison of *The Handmaid's Tale* and one other suitable text, analyse how the ideas of conformity and rebellion are explored by the writers.
- Sometimes the overview is provided by genre:
  Comedy is often used by writers to convey judgements. Compare two appropriate texts to explore this idea.
- The question might be based on a series of unseen extracts and your own reading on the subject, with a focus on the idea of genre or 'typicality':
  Using the extracts provided and with reference to your own reading, examine how typical these writings are of First World War literature.

So, to sum up, all this means that you may have to consider answering questions on:
- paired texts
- clusters or groups of texts built around a central theme
- a range of your own chosen texts to contextualise the key text(s)

Make sure that you are clear which of these you are going to be asked to do, and prepare carefully.